I0818564

ON THE HUNT
DEER
HUNTING
BY ROXANNE TROUP
EPIC
BELLWETHER MEDIA • MINNEAPOLIS, MN

EPIC

EPIC BOOKS are no ordinary books. They burst with intense action, high-speed heroics, and shadows of the unknown. Are you ready for an Epic adventure?

This edition first published in 2025 by Bellwether Media, Inc.

No part of this publication may be reproduced in whole or in part without written permission of the publisher. For information regarding permission, write to Bellwether Media, Inc., Attention: Permissions Department, 6012 Blue Circle Drive, Minnetonka, MN 55343.

Library of Congress Cataloging-in-Publication Data

LC record for Deer Hunting available at: https://lccn.loc.gov/2024037676

Editor: Elizabeth Neuenfeldt Designer: Jeffrey Kollock

Printed in the United States of America, North Mankato, MN.

TABLE OF CONTENTS

WAITING FOR DAWN

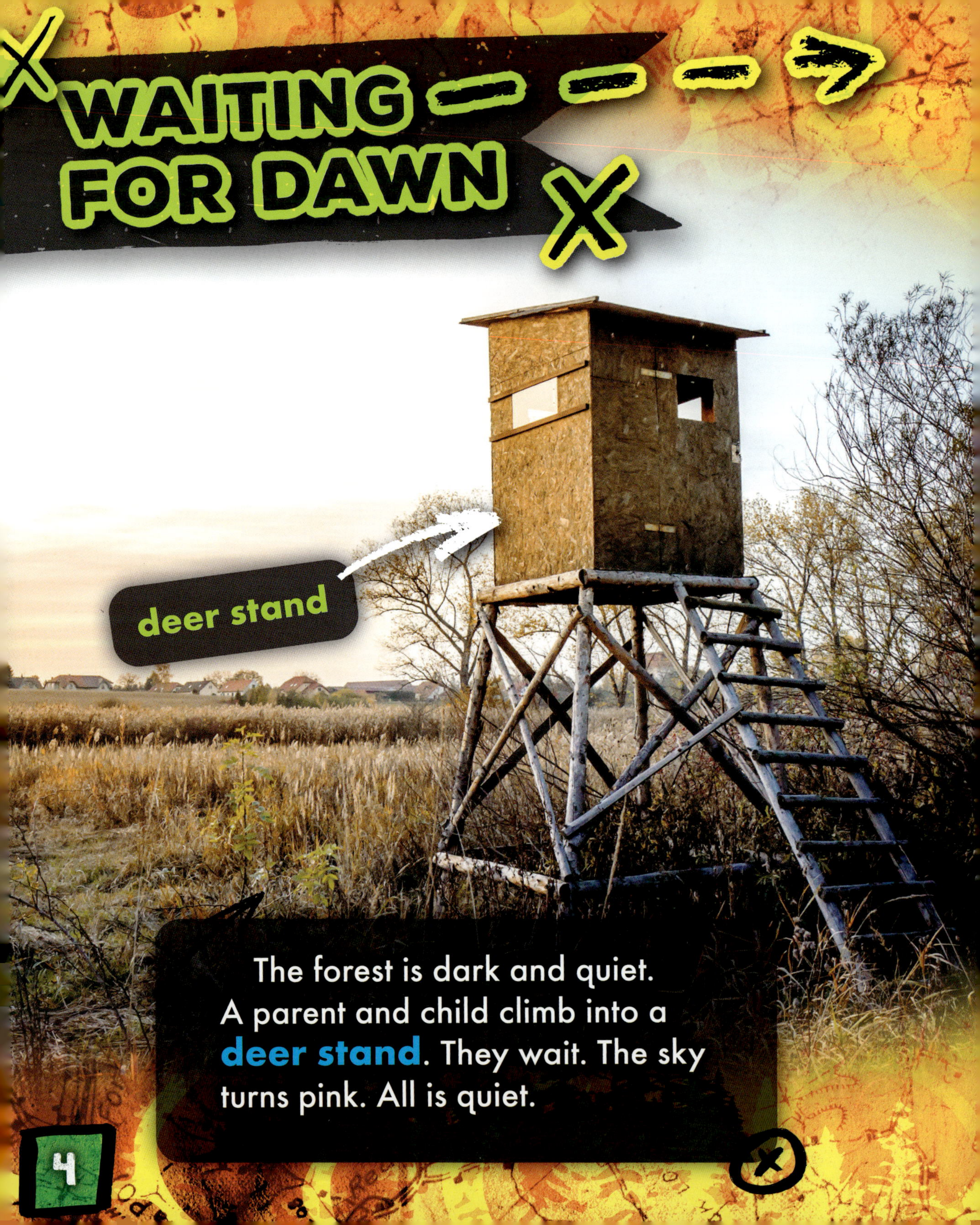

The forest is dark and quiet. A parent and child climb into a **deer stand**. They wait. The sky turns pink. All is quiet.

Suddenly, a deer parades through the trees. The child points. It is a **buck**!

WHAT IS DEER HUNTING?

Deer have many uses. Some people hunt for food. Others turn **hides** into leather. They make tools from **antlers**.

Many hunters like being outdoors. They enjoy being with family and friends.

Deer hunting season often takes place each fall in North America.

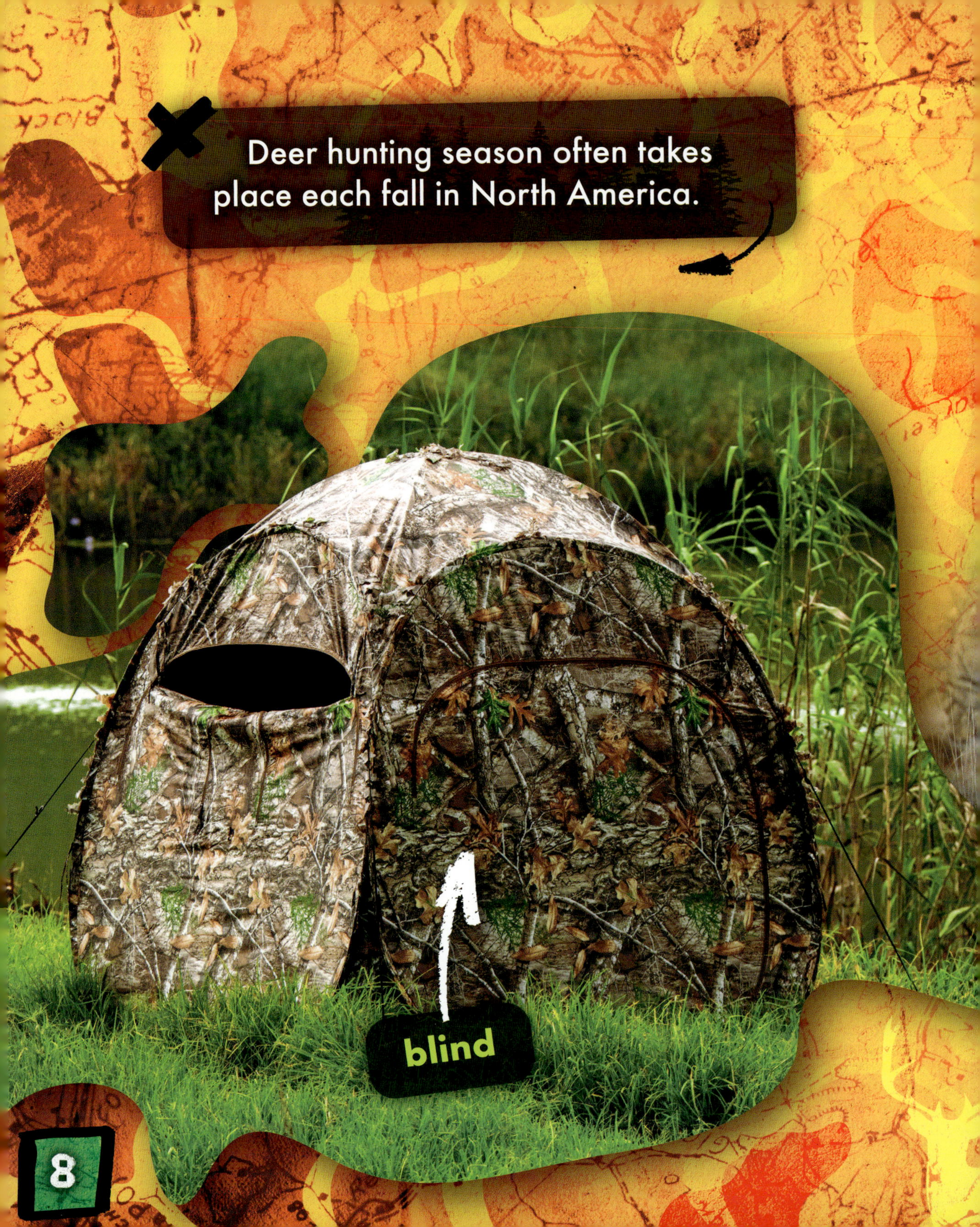

In forests, hunters wait in deer stands or **blinds**. Raised deer stands help hunters see far. Blinds help hunters hide. On **prairies**, hunters **stalk** deer.

Deer hunting helps deer numbers. Too many deer in one area can limit food for other animals. Deer can spread diseases.

States track the health of their deer. They plan hunting seasons to keep herds healthy.

TIME TO HUNT

Deer hunting season in the United States is planned by each state. In some states, deer hunting season lasts for months. In other states, it may last around a week!

PREPARING TO HUNT

Deer have strong senses. Odd sounds, smells, and movements scare them away.

Hunters stay silent and still. They wear camouflage to stay hidden.
camouflage
HEARING SUPERPOWER
Deer turn their ears individually. They can hear sound in every direction without moving their heads!

Hunters cover their heads and chests in **blaze orange**. Deer cannot see the color. But other hunters can. This keeps everyone safe.

Hunters wear layers to stay warm and dry. They wear hats and sturdy boots.

Most deer hunters use a rifle and **scope**. This allows hunters to shoot from far away.

HUNTING GEAR

Some hunters use a bow and arrow to hunt. Bow hunters must get close to the deer.

RULES OF THE HUNT

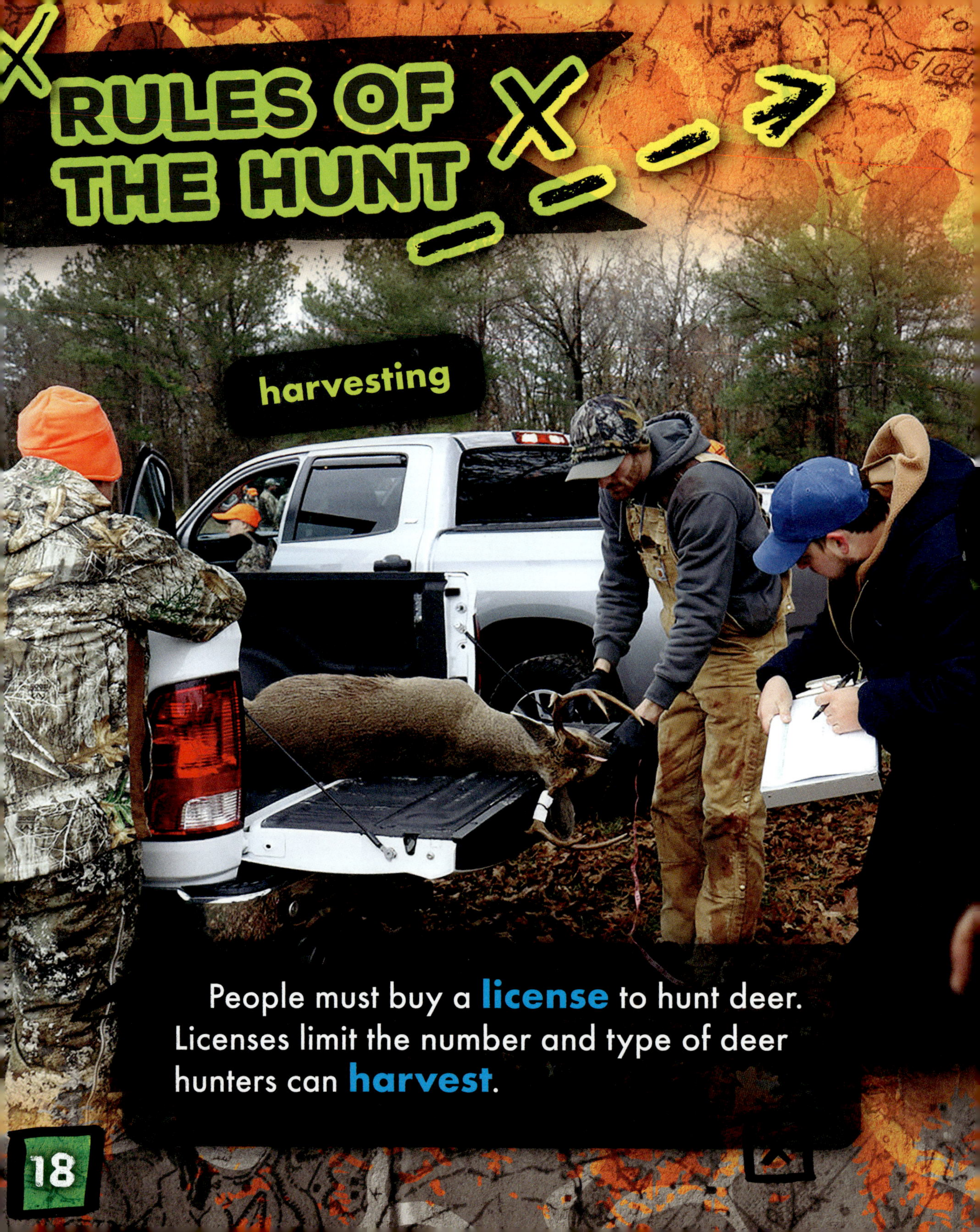

People must buy a **license** to hunt deer. Licenses limit the number and type of deer hunters can **harvest**.

The money hunters spend supports **conservation** and education.

Most states require hunters to take a safety class before hunting.

The class shares local laws and gun safety. It also teaches **ethical shot** placement. It keeps deer hunting safe and fun!

hunting safety class

ethical shot placement

GLOSSARY

antlers—branched horns that grow on male deer

blaze orange—a bright orange color that hunters wear for safety

blinds—small huts or closed spaces in which hunters wait

buck—a male deer

camouflage—a fabric that uses colors and patterns to blend in with surroundings

conservation—taking care of the environment

deer stand—a raised platform on which hunters wait and watch for deer

ethical shot—a clean shot that reduces pain and suffering to an animal

harvest—collect

hides—deer skins

license—a document that gives hunters legal permission to harvest a certain type of animal

prairies—large grasslands that are mostly flat and treeless

scope—a small telescope attached to a gun; a scope helps hunters see their targets from far away.

stalk—to follow quietly and carefully

AT THE LIBRARY

Doyle, Abby Badach. *Deer Hunting*. New York, N.Y.: Gareth Stevens Publishing, 2023.

Scheffer, Janie. *White-tailed Deer*. Minneapolis, Minn.: Bellwether Media, 2025.

Troup, Roxanne. *Elk Hunting*. Minneapolis, Minn.: Bellwether Media, 2025.

ON THE WEB

Factsurfer.com gives you a safe, fun way to find more information.

1. Go to www.factsurfer.com.
2. Enter "deer hunting" into the search box and click 🔍.
3. Select your book cover to see a list of related content.

INDEX

The images in this book are reproduced through the courtesy of: Jim Cumming, cover; Ray Hennessy, p. 3; Petr Svoboda, p. 4; Tom Reichner, p. 5; North Wind Picture Archives/ Alamy, p. 6; Warren Price Photography, p. 6 (hide leather); Design Pics Inc/ Alamy, p. 7; Roman Kybus, p. 7 (antler tool); Robert Wedderburn, p. 8; Steve Oehlenschlager, p. 9; Dennis W Donohue, p. 9 (deer); Bruce MacQueen, p. 11; critterbiz, p. 12; paul geilfuss, p. 13; CSNafzger, p. 14; Katelyn Sjostrand, p. 14 (blaze orange); RJ_Cooper, p. 15; Nathan Allred/ Alamy, p. 16; muroPhotographer, p. 17; SolidMaks, p. 17 (rifle, ammo); rustycanuck, p. 17 (blaze orange); Nikita Rogul, p. 17 (camouflage); piemags/PL Photography Limited, p. 18; Tribune Content Agency LLC/ Alamy, p. 19; Kozup Photography, p. 20; Ricardo Reitmeyer, p. 21; Stephen Bonk, p. 21 (inset); Tochanchai, p. 23.